My
g
Book

by Jane Belk Moncure
illustrated by Linda Hohag

THE CHILD'S WORLD

ELGIN, ILLINOIS 60120

Library of Congress Cataloging in Publication Data

Moncure, Jane Belk.
  My "g" book.

  (My first steps to reading)
  Rev. ed. of: My g sound box. © 1979.
  Summary: Little g goes into the garden and finds many
things that begin with hard "g" to put in her box.
  1. Children's stories, American.   [1. Alphabet]
I. Hohag, Linda. ill.   II. Moncure, Jane Belk.   My g sound
box.   III. Title.   IV. Series: Moncure, Jane Belk.   My
first steps to reading.
PZ7.M739Myg   1984   [E]   84-17547
ISBN 0-89565-281-1

Distributed by Childrens Press, 1224 West Van Buren Street,
Chicago, Illinois 60607.

My "g" Book

(This book uses only the hard "g" sound in the story line. Blends are included.
Words beginning with the soft "g" sound are included at the end of the book.)

Little g had a box.

She said, "I will fill my box."

She opened the gate and
went into the garden.

Little found goats in the garden.

"In you go, goats," she said.

Then she  found grass,

lots of green grass.

She put some grass into her box.

But the goats ate the grass.

Then she found grapes,

lots of grapes.

She put the grapes into her box.

But the goats ate the grapes too.

What could Little  g do?

She found a gorilla.

She put the gorilla into her box.

Did the goats eat the gorilla? No.

The goats grinned.

The gorilla grinned.

Little  found a guitar.

She played the guitar.

The goats danced

with the gorilla.

Everyone giggled.

Little g found glasses. She put glasses on the goats.

Then she found goggles.

She put goggles on the gorilla.

Just then a goose and
gander walked by.

"What funny goats.
What a funny gorilla,"
said the goose and gander.

Little g caught them.
"I will put you into
my box," she said.

"I will give you a gift,"
said the goose.

She laid an egg made of gold. "What a great g gift," said Little g.

Little  looked around.

guitar

grapes

gander

egg of gold

goose

"What a great group of "g's," she said.

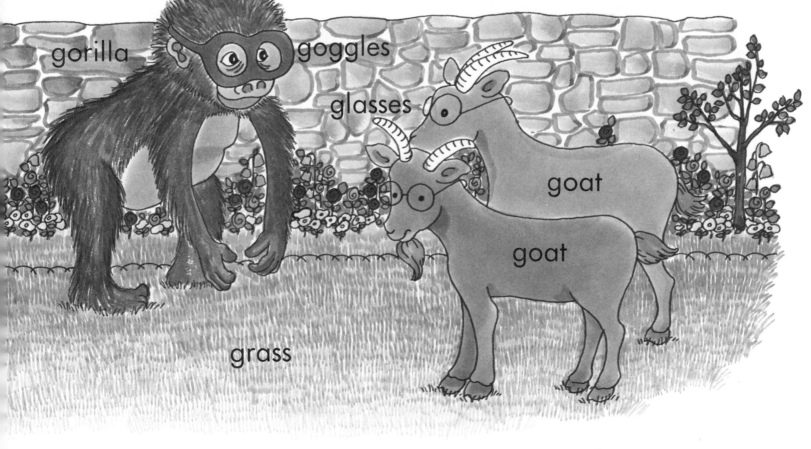

gorilla

goggles

glasses

goat

goat

grass

More words with Little g.

gum

goldfish

gull

glass

globe

gumdrop

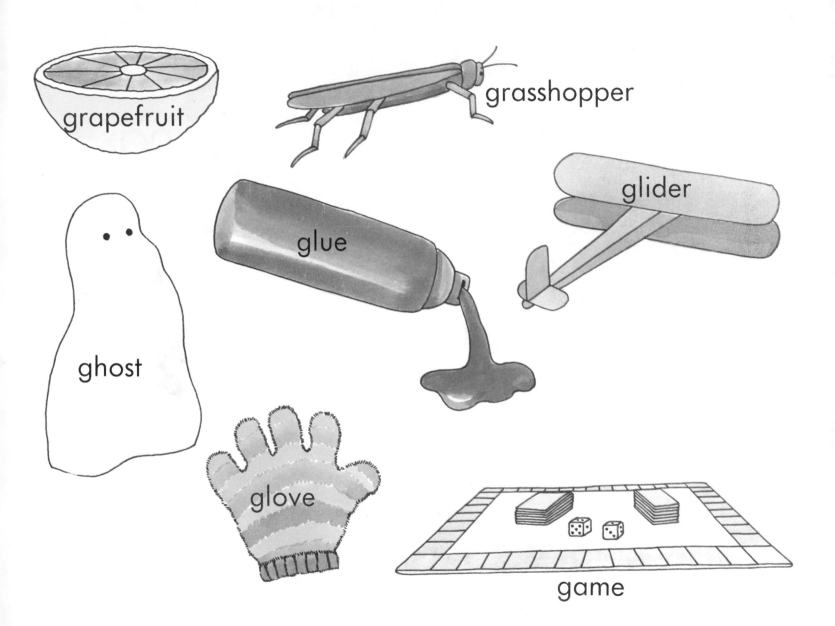

grapefruit

grasshopper

glider

ghost

glue

glove

game

In this story, Little g has a hard "g" sound.

Little g has another sound too. It is like the sound of the letter "j."

Read these words. Listen for the softer sound.